Buddha

Published by Roaring Brook Press
Roaring Brook Press is a division of Holtzbrinck Publishing Holdings Limited Partnership
175 Fifth Avenue, New York, NY 10010
mackids.com

Library of Congress Control Number: 2018944879
ISBN 978-1-250-16888-7

Our books may be purchased in bulk for promotional, educational, or business use. Please contact your local bookseller or the Macmillan Corporate and Premium Sales Department at (800) 221-7945 ext. 5442 or by email at MacmillanSpecialMarkets@macmillan.com.

First published in France in 2014 by Quelle Histoire, Paris
First U.S. edition, 2019

Text: Patricia Crété
Translation: Catherine Nolan
Illustrations: Bruno Wennagel, Mathieu Ferret

Printed in Hong Kong by RR Donnelley Asia Printing Solutions Ltd.

10 9 8 7 6 5 4 3 2 1

Buddha

Roaring Brook Press
New York

Birth of the Buddha

The Buddha was an important spiritual leader. An entire religion—Buddhism—is based on his teachings. Not much is known about his life. Most of the information about him is a mix of legend and history.

It is believed that he was born more than two thousand years ago in the village of Lumbini, Nepal. His mother gave birth to him under a tree while flowers rained down from the sky. She placed him in a white lotus—a sacred flower. Then she named him Siddhartha, which means "he who reaches his goal."

The Prince's Youth

Siddhartha's father was the king of Kosala, a small kingdom at the foot of the Himalayan mountains. Siddhartha grew up in a castle, where teachers gave him lessons in science, literature, and foreign languages. He also practiced sports, including archery, horseback riding, and fencing, as well as studied music and dance.

A Hindu priest, called a *Brahman*, introduced Siddhartha to the mysteries of religion.

Marriage to Yasodhara

When Siddhartha turned sixteen, his father decided he should get married. Many young women came to meet him, including a princess named Yasodhara. Like Siddhartha, she was sixteen years old. She was very pretty. He fell in love with her immediately, and they soon wed.

Ten years later, they had a baby boy named Rahula.

Leaving the Palace

Siddhartha had a good life, but he grew restless. One morning, he left his palace and began exploring.

He met three wise men who taught him valuable lessons. Siddhartha knew that he had much more to learn. He decided not to go back home. Instead, he would journey on to find true happiness.

A New Life

Siddhartha cut his hair and sent away his servants. He traveled alone to the city of Gaya in India where there was a busy shrine dedicated to the Hindu god Vishnu.

But Siddhartha slipped away to a quiet cave. There, he began to meditate. He hardly ate or slept, and he stayed in the same position for hours without moving.

Siddhartha kept this up for six years. One day, he collapsed. He was nearly starved! A young girl found him and gave him food. She saved his life.

Becoming the Buddha

Siddhartha left Gaya and went to the village of Uruvela. He stopped near a large fig tree. He walked around it seven times, then sat down on some straw with his legs crossed and began to meditate again. He stayed like this for seven days and seven nights.

Finally, he woke up full of joy. He had reached enlightenment. That meant he had found peace and a deep understanding of the universe.

From then on, Siddhartha was called the Buddha, which means "the awakened one."

First Lesson

The Buddha wanted to help other people become wiser and better. He wanted to teach them what was important in life and what was not.

The Buddha gave his first lesson in a village called Sarnath to an audience of young people. They wrote down everything he said. This sermon of Sarnath became the first Buddhist text.

Teaching and Traveling

The Buddha spent the next forty-five years preaching. He trekked many miles a day, sharing his knowledge. Everyone from princes to peasants listened to him, including the wife and son he had left behind.

Some of the Buddha's listeners formed communities where people could practice Buddhism together. Others followed him on his travels and became his disciples.

Last Days

The Buddha turned eighty years old. He walked slowly, leaning on a stick.

The Buddha set out for the place where he was born, but he was too tired. He became ill along the way, in a place called Kushinagar. He lay down in the forest between two trees. He died there, in the middle of nature, with his disciples around him.

The Buddha's Legacy

Even though the Buddha was gone, his ideas lived on. Buddhism spread across India and the rest of Asia. In the twentieth century, many people in the Western world, including America, began following Buddhism, too.

The Buddha's words and wisdom inspired people around the globe.

570 BC

563 BC
Siddhartha is
born.

563 BC
Siddhartha's
mother dies.

547 BC
Siddhartha
meets
Yasodhara,
who becomes
his wife.

537 BC
Siddhartha's
son, Rahula,
is born.

534 BC
Siddhartha
leaves his
palace and
begins his
journey.

528 BC
Siddhartha finds enlightenment and becomes the Buddha.

528–483 BC
The Buddha travels all over India, preaching.

483 BC
The Buddha dies.

480 BC

528 BC
Siddhartha nearly starves to death while fasting and meditating. A young girl saves him by giving him food.

528 BC
In Sarnath, the Buddha gives his first lesson.

All dates are approximate.

Buddha's Journey

1 Lumbini, Nepal

Many pilgrims travel to the Buddha's birthplace to pay tribute to him.

2 Kapilavastu, Nepal

Archaeologists found the remains of a large palace here that belonged to the Buddha's family. Kapilavastu is located near the border between India and Nepal.

3 Gaya, India

The Buddha visited a temple in Gaya that was dedicated to the Hindu god Vishnu. Thousands of people visit the temple every year.

4 Uruvela, India

Siddhartha reached enlightenment in Uruvela under a sacred fig tree. It is one of the most famous places connected with Buddhism. A temple called Mahabodhi was built here in approximately 260 BC.

5 Sarnath, India

The Buddha delivered his first sermon in Sarnath, in northern India.

6 Kushinagar, India

Kushinagar is located near the Nepalese border, close to Kapilavastu, Nepal, where Siddhartha's family lived. The Buddha died here, with his disciples around him.

People to Know

Mayadevi

Mayadevi, also known as Queen Maya, was Siddhartha's mother. She died a few days after her son was born.

Mara the Demon

Legend has it that while Siddhartha was meditating under the tree in Uruvela, a demon named Mara tried to distract him by causing a hurricane.

Alexander Cunningham

(1814–1893)

This British archaeologist was only a young man when he discovered the ruins of Sarnath: a temple, a monastery, and other important buildings erected at the location of the Buddha's first sermon.

The Dalai Lama

The Dalai Lama is the highest religious leader for Tibetan Buddhists. He is also the Tibetan head of state.

....

One of the Buddha's teeth is held in a temple in Sri Lanka called the Temple of the Sacred Tooth.

....

Scriptures describe the Buddha as very handsome, with a strong jaw and long eyelashes. He was also said to have a deep voice.

Though the Buddha founded one of the world's major religions, he never thought of himself as a religious leader and had a fairly small following when he was alive.

Many people who follow Buddhism avoid eating meat as part of their religion. But the Buddha himself was not a vegetarian.

Available Now

 Muhammad Ali
 Marie Antoinette
 Neil Armstrong
 Blackbeard
 Buddha
 Coco Chanel
 Charlie Chaplin

 Cleopatra
 Marie Curie
 Albert Einstein
 Anne Frank
 Gandhi
 Frida Kahlo
 Martin Luther King Jr.

 Abraham Lincoln
 Nelson Mandela
 Isaac Newton
 Rosa Parks
 Pocahontas
 Vincent van Gogh

Coming Soon

 Joan of Arc
 John F. Kennedy
 Pablo Picasso
 Princess Diana